D1383312

Community Helpers

Food Service
Workers

by **Debbie L. Yanuck**

Consultant:
William Vear
Senior Director of Education
Texas Restaurant Association Education Foundation

Bridgestone Books
an imprint of Capstone Press
Mankato, Minnesota

A 4-8

Bridgestone Books are published by Capstone Press
151 Good Counsel Drive, P.O. Box 669, Mankato, Minnesota 56002
http://www.capstone-press.com

Library of Congress Cataloging-in-Publication Data
Yanuck, Debbie L.
    Food service workers/by Debbie L. Yanuck.
    p. cm.—(Community helpers)
    Includes bibliographical references and index.
    Summary: A simple introduction to the work food service workers do, discussing
where they work and how they are important to the communities they serve.
    ISBN 0-7368-1128-1
    1. Food service—Juvenile literature. [1. Food service. 2.Occupations.] I. Title.
II. Community helpers (Mankato, Minn.)
TX943 .Y36 2002
647.95'023—dc21   2001003325

Editorial Credits
Megan Schoeneberger, editor; Karen Risch, product planning editor; Linda Clavel, cover
    production designer, Katy Kudela, photo researcher

Photo Credits
Capstone Press/Gregg Andersen, cover; Gary Sundermeyer, 4, 10
Leslie O'Shaughnessy, 18, 20
Matt Lindsay/Photophile, 8
Photri-Microstock/Jeff Greenberg, 16
Shaffer Photography/James L. Shaffer, 12, 14
Visuals Unlimited/Jeff Greenberg, 6

1 2 3 4 5 6 07 06 05 04 03 02

Table of Contents

Fresh
PIZZA
Fresh
PIZZA
Fresh
PIZZA
Free Delivery
Fresh, Hot, and Fast!

Food Service Workers

Food service workers serve food and beverages. They work in places where people pay to eat meals. Waiters and waitresses, cafeteria workers, and fast-food workers are types of food service workers.

beverage
a drink

What Food Service Workers Do

Food service workers help customers at restaurants or cafeterias. They sometimes greet customers and seat them at tables. Food service workers ask customers what they want to eat and drink. They also figure out how much customers owe for their food.

customer
a person who buys goods or services

Waiters and Waitresses

Waiters and waitresses work in restaurants. They make sure customers have menus. Waiters and waitresses answer questions or tell how the food is prepared. They take food orders and bring food to customers. They sometimes offer desserts and coffee.

menu
a list of food and drinks
served at a restaurant

Cafeteria Workers

Cafeteria workers serve food in school or hospital cafeterias. They often stand behind counters. Cafeteria food is cooked ahead of time and placed on warmers. Cafeteria workers serve food from the warmers onto trays or plates.

Fast-Food Workers

Fast-food workers work in fast-food restaurants. They take orders from behind counters. Fast-food workers also serve customers at drive-through windows. Some fast-food workers also wipe tables, mop floors, and empty trash cans.

Skills Food Service Workers Need

Food service workers need good math skills to add up prices. They sometimes use cash registers or computers. Food service workers need to remember orders. Food service workers should enjoy working with people. They should be friendly and polite.

cash register
a machine that records, counts, and holds money

15

People Who Help Food Service Workers

Many people help food service workers do their jobs. Executive chefs are in charge of the kitchen. Chefs prepare and cook food. Kitchen helpers wash and dry dishes. Hosts and hostesses sometimes seat people at tables and hand out menus. Dining room helpers clear and set tables.

Other Food Service Jobs

Some food service workers do not serve food. Managers order supplies such as plates, glasses, and napkins. They hire new workers. Managers or executive chefs plan menus and decide prices. Accountants keep track of how much money a restaurant makes.

manager
someone who is in charge of a business

How Food Service Workers Help Others

Food service workers help people by serving them food. They serve lunches to students and teachers. They serve meals to people in hospital cafeterias. Waiters and waitresses bring food to customers in restaurants.

Hands On: Serve a Meal

Food service workers need to be polite and friendly. They sometimes help in the kitchen. You can be a food service worker and serve a meal to your family.

What You Need

Pencil
Paper

What You Do

1. Write down what is being served for dinner on a piece of paper. This will be your menu for dinner.
2. Seat your family at the table. Offer them a beverage such as milk or juice.
3. Pour the beverages they ordered into their cups.
4. Tell your family what is on the menu for dinner. Find out what each person wants from the menu.
5. With an adult helping you, prepare a plate of food for each member of your family. See if you can remember what each person ordered.
6. Serve the food.

Food service workers often clear dirty dishes and wipe the table after customers leave. Help your family clean the table after the meal.

Words to Know

accountant (uh-KOUN-tuhnt)—someone who keeps track of money at a business

cafeteria (kaf-uh-TIHR-ee-uh)—a place where customers serve themselves or are served at a counter

counter (KOUN-tur)—a long, flat surface; cafeteria and fast-food workers often stand behind counters.

executive chef (eg-ZEK-yuh-tiv SHEF)—a restaurant cook who is in charge of the kitchen and often helps plan the menu

hire (HIRE)—to give someone a job

menu (MEN-yoo)—a list of foods and drinks served in a restaurant

restaurant (RESS-tuh-rahnt)—a place where people pay to eat meals

Read More

Beal, Eileen. *Choosing a Career in the Restaurant Industry.* World of Work. New York: Rosen, 1999.

Klingel, Cynthia Fitterer, and Robert B. Noyed. *School Cafeteria Workers.* My School Helpers. Vero Beach, Fla.: Rourke, 2001.

Internet Sites

FDA/CFSAN For Kids, Teens, and Educators
http://www.cfsan.fda.gov/~dms/educate.html
Waiters and Waitresses
http://icpac.indiana.edu/careers/career_profiles/100223.xml

Index